LARGE PRINT

READ ALOUD
ANCIENT TALES

How Parvati became Durga
and other stories...

ANURAG MEHTA

Nita Mehta Publications
Enriching Young Minds

LARGE PRINT
READ ALOUD
ANCIENT TALES
How Parvati became Durga and other stories...

Nita Mehta Publications

Corporate Office
3A/3, Asaf Ali Road, New Delhi 110 002
Phone: +91 11 2325 2948, 2325 0091
E-mail: nitamehta@nitamehta.com
Website: www.nitamehta.com

© Copyright NITA MEHTA PUBLICATIONS 2014
All rights reserved
ISBN 978-81-7676-151-2

First Print 2014

Printed in India at Infinity Advertising Services (P) Ltd, New Delhi

Editorial and Marketing office
E-159, Greater Kailash II, New Delhi 110 048

Cover Designed by: **flyingtrees**

Typesetting by National Information Technology Academy
3A/3, Asaf Ali Road, New Delhi 110 002

Distributed by :
NITA MEHTA BOOKS
3A/3, Asaf Ali Road, New Delhi - 02

Distribution Centre :
D16/1, Okhla Industrial Area, Phase-I,
New Delhi - 110020
Tel.: 26813199, 26813200
E-mail: nitamehta.mehta@gmail.com

Contributing Writers:
Subhash Mehta
Tanya Mehta

Editorial & Proofreading:
Rajesh
Ramesh

WORLD RIGHTS RESERVED: The contents - all text, photographs and drawings are original and copyrighted. No portion of this book shall be reproduced, stored in a retrieval system or transmitted by any means, electronic, mechanical, photocopying, recording or otherwise, without the written permission of the publishers. While every precaution is taken in the preparation of this book, the publishers and the author assume no responsibility for errors or omissions. Neither is any liability assumed for damages resulting from the use of information contained herein. TRADEMARKS ACKNOWLEDGED: Trademarks used, if any, are acknowledged as trademarks of their respective owners. These are used as reference only and no trademark infringement is intended upon.

Price: Rs. 145/-   US $ 6.95   UK £ 3.95

CONTENTS

The Horse Headed Asura   4

The Dwarf Conqueror   8

The Story of Mahakaleshwar Temple   14

The Descent of Ganga   18

The Princess and the Three Suitors   24

How Parvati became Durga?   31

Brahma's Lie   36

Hanuman Gets the Sacred Herb   40

THE HORSE HEADED ASURA

"I want to be immortal," Hayagriva, the horse headed Asura, requested Brahma. "That is not possible," Brahma sagely shook his head as he reclined on his celestial seat.

"Then please allow me this boon," Hayagriva uttered plaintively, "allow me to be killed only by the one, who also has a horse-head like me."

Brahma unthinkingly granted the boon. What Brahma did not realize that Hayagriva was one of a kind. There was no one like him, in the entire cosmos!

Thus, he believed that he could not be killed. Naturally, undeterred, Hayagriva created havoc everywhere. In fact, with evil intent, Hayagriva stole one Veda from Brahma too. Desperately, the Devas rushed to Lord Brahma for help.

"Ask Lord Vishnu. He will surely help you," advised Lord Brahma.

When the Devas reached, they saw Lord Vishnu in a deep slumber.

Vishnu was sleeping with his head resting over his bow. In the spur of the moment, the Devas devised a plan.

As planned, they sent termites to powder the bow. Oh dear, as soon as the wood of the bow was eaten, the bowstring broke so hard that the pressure sliced Vishnu's neck!

The Devas immediately attached a horse's head on Vishnu's severed neck.

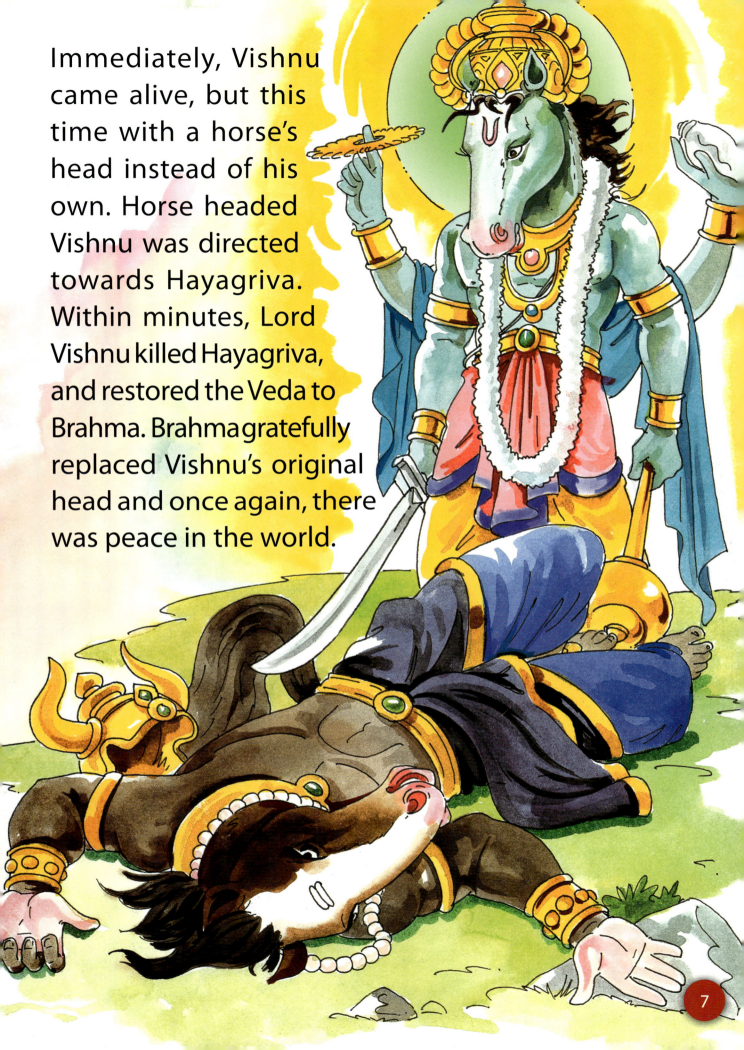

Immediately, Vishnu came alive, but this time with a horse's head instead of his own. Horse headed Vishnu was directed towards Hayagriva. Within minutes, Lord Vishnu killed Hayagriva, and restored the Veda to Brahma. Brahma gratefully replaced Vishnu's original head and once again, there was peace in the world.

THE DWARF CONQUEROR

Thousands of years ago, Bali, the demon king, expanded his kingdom in all directions. Nearly, the whole world came under his rule.

As Bali's power increased, the gods became worried.

"At this rate, he will soon snatch our kingdom. It will be the rule of the demons then. Where will we go ?" the gods complained to Lord Vishnu.

"Don't worry," answered Vishnu, "I'll go to Bali's kingdom as a dwarf."

"As a dwarf?" the gods wondered aloud.

Vishnu smiled and then vanished.

Very soon, Vishnu was born to a Brahmin couple. He did not grow like most children. Instead, his height stopped at the age of seven, turning him into a dwarf.

One day, Vishnu visited the palace of King Bali, with the intention of asking for alms.

"Alms for the poor Brahmin," the dwarf chanted, spreading one hand before the tall and hefty Bali. King Bali had just stepped out of his palace. Bali was very amused to see this confident dwarf.

Hiding his amusement, Bali asked, "So little one, what do you want?"

Before the dwarf could speak, the royal priest rushed from his seat and stood between Bali and the dwarf.

"Your royal highness, don't fall for this trick. The little VAMANA (Dwarf) has come to conquer you. He is Lord Vishnu."

"Vishnu! So small?" laughed Bali, ignoring the priest. He turned towards the dwarf and repeated, "Yes, little Vamana, what do you want?"

"I am small and my needs are small. I wish to live on my own land. All I ask for is a piece of land, which I can cover in three steps," the dwarf demanded politely.

"Don't listen to him! I am warning you," the royal priest frantically intervened, but Bali brushed him aside.

"Is that all? Just three steps?" asked Bali. When the Vamana nodded, Bali announced, "Very well! Take your three steps."

"Shall I?" asked Vishnu in the form of Vamana.

"Yes, of course," nodded Bali fearlessly.

The next moment, heavenly music rang and fragrance of thousands of jasmine flowers floated in the air. The little Vamana grew into the celestial stature of Vishnu.

Vishnu took his FIRST step and covered the whole earth. In his SECOND step, he covered the heavens. Vishnu's THIRD step landed on the head of Bali pushing him down under, into Patal Lok (the underworld).

This way once again the kingdom of the gods was rescued from the threat of demons and the people were saved from demon rule.

THE STORY OF MAHAKALESHWAR TEMPLE

Long, long ago, in the city of Ujjain, the rule of the demons made it impossible for people to pray to the Gods.

Demon King Dushan declared, "I will kill anyone who recites the vedas or prays to Shiva!"

This badly affected the brahmins. One such family of brahmins lived in Ujjain. Devpriya, Sukrit, Priyamedha and Suvrat were brothers. They were devout disciples of Shiva. They prayed to Shiva and recited Vedas, not caring for the ban. "Om Namah Shivay! Om Namah Shivay," the brahmin brothers chanted loudly in front of a Shivling.

Dushan was furious when he saw the brothers praying devoutly to the Shivling.

"STOP!" Dushan raised his sword to interrupt them.

"MRRRREARRR!!!"

A loud sound erupted, halting his actions. Horrified, Dushan stepped back. The Shivling was sinking into the ground; making a huge crater as it went! Before anyone could react, with a dramatic whoosh, Shiva emerged from the innards of the crater.

With an angry roar, Shiva wiped Dushan and his demons from the face of the earth! The spot where Shiva vanquished the demons was by the banks of the Shipra River, flowing through the city of Ujjain.

A temple was built at that place. It is called the Mahakaleshwar temple.

THE DESCENT OF GANGA

Ganga was the elder daughter of Queen Mena and King Himavan. She lived in heaven and Ganga's mystic quality of cleansing everything she touched, was really appreciated and talked about.

However, things were not so happy down below, on earth. During this period, King Sagar was performing the holy Ashvamedha yagna. A sacred horse was supposed to be left free to roam the world. If the horse came back unopposed, the extent of territory he covered, would become that of the king performing the yagna. But a mishap prevented the yagna from continuing. Before the horse could be set free, he was lost! Anxiously, King Sagar's sixty thousand sons went out in search of the lost animal. They eventually found the horse grazing at sage Kapil Muni's ashram.

The sons thought that Kapil Muni had deliberately taken the horse. Without waiting for any explanations, they hurled abuses at the sage. The innocent Kapil Muni, was furious. Kapil Muni, by the force of his prayers, was very powerful. With one fiery glare, he burnt Sagar's sixty thousand sons to ashes.

Since they had been killed this way, it was believed that the spirits of the sixty thousands sons of Sagar would wander helplessly in the under worlds. Generations of King Sagar's kin tried to undo the curse. But failed! Finally, it was Prince Bhagirath, two centuries later, who through hard penance to Shiva got some success.

"O lord, have mercy on my ancestors! Show me a way to undo the curse."

"I will have to ask Ganga to descend on earth. The purity of Ganga's touch, on the ashes, can only wash away the curse over Sagar's sons," Shiva answered.

"Oh, I would love to visit earth," Ganga eagerly agreed when she was asked.

Ganga was in the presence of Shiva, Vishnu and Brahma at that moment.

"But, if Ganga descends, her force will split the young earth into two. Earth will surely perish," warned Brahma, when he heard about the whole thing.

Shiva had a solution to that problem too. As Ganga prepared her descent, Shiva trapped her in his matted locks, allowing her to flow out in streams. This way Shiva broke the force of her fall!

As Ganga spread on earth, her purifying powers were doubly blessed with the touch of Shiva. Meandering through the plains, Ganga reached the place where the ashes lay. She washed away the curse and granted them salvation.

Ganga sanctified many cities by flowing through them. Eventually, she flowed into the sea.

THE PRINCESS AND THE THREE SUITORS

Once a Princess named Mithili was unable to decide who to marry! Three very eligible bachelor Princes approached her father for her hand. The first prince was called Nalin. Prince Nalin apart from being extremely good looking, had powers that enabled him to understand a situation through visions. The second prince was Vishal who besides being handsome, owned a chariot that could fly! Similarly, the third prince named Ajith was not only handsome but also very strong.

Prince Nalin

He was so strong that he could behead anyone with one stroke of his sword!

Well, since the King could not decide who was the best out of the three, he decided, "Let my daughter Mithili choose whom she wants to marry."

He threw a grand reception and invited the three eligible grooms, for this purpose.

Prince Vishal

Prince Ajith

When all the guests had arrived, the king ordered a courtier to call his daughter to the reception area.

The courtier sprinted back, gasping, "The Princess is not in her room. *The Princess has vanished!*"

This news shocked the guests. A search party was sent out to look for her. They returned disappointed.

Princess Mithili had simply disappeared! Suddenly, Prince Nalin spoke,

"Princess Mithili has been captured by the giant Asura (demon) residing at the high mountain top, as per my vision."

"Come, let us go there in my flying carriage," the second prince, Vishal, urged Nalin, Ajith and the King.

Thus, they flew to the mountain top. As earlier determined by Nalin, Mithili had *in fact been* captured by the giant Asura. Gloating over his prize, the gigantic Asura laughed as he *stood behind the mountain*.

Poor Princess Mithili had been pushed into a natural hollow gap of the mountain. She was sitting there looking very sad.

"Yaaaaargh," the Asura threw flames from his mouth. The chariot rocked crazily. With great concentration, Ajith managed to jump off the chariot and on to the mountain peak. He stood on the mountain peak and challenged the demonic Asura.

Surprised at the tiny company, Asura bent his head, peering closely at Ajith. That was all Ajith needed. With one clean stroke of his sword, he beheaded the colossal Asura. Mithili was saved and soon safely soared back to her kingdom. But now, another problem arose. Of the three princes, whom should princess Mithili marry?

When Mithili was asked this, she immediately replied, "Prince Ajith, of course."

Her father asked her the reason for choosing Ajith. "Ajith actually faced the Asura and saved my life. He is very brave. The others managed things from afar."

The king applauded his daughter's choice and the princess married Ajith.

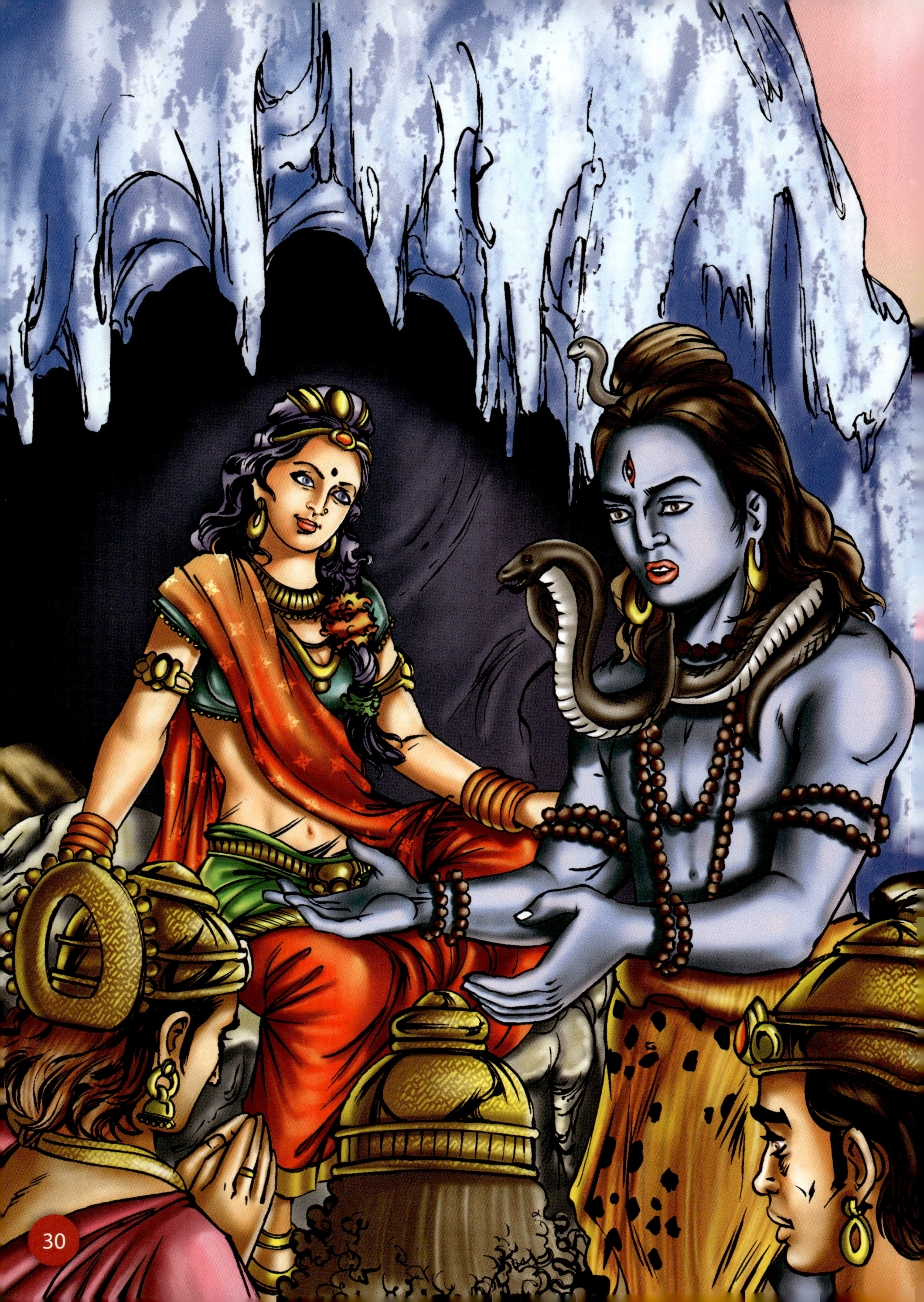

HOW PARVATI BECAME DURGA?

Goddess Parvati, wife of Lord Shiva, is a loving and docile mother and wife. However, there is another form that Parvati takes. That is of Durga. As Durga, she becomes a powerful warrior. From this form of Durga, she takes many other forms for the destruction of demons who are troubling Gods and mankind. How did she get the name Durga?

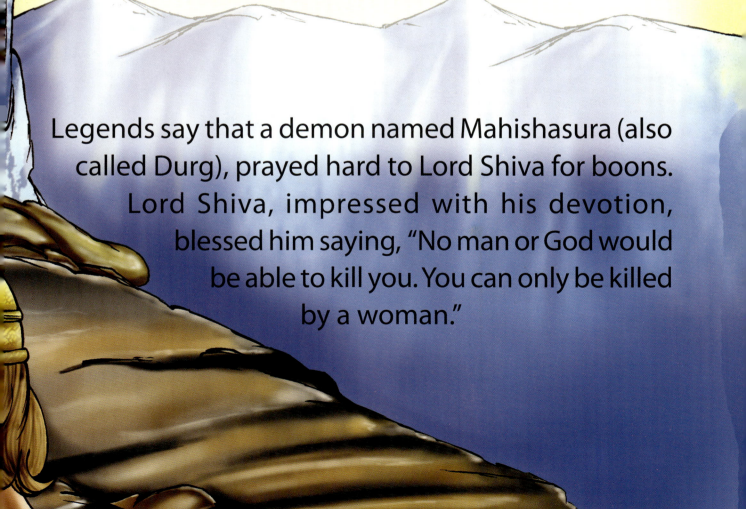

Legends say that a demon named Mahishasura (also called Durg), prayed hard to Lord Shiva for boons. Lord Shiva, impressed with his devotion, blessed him saying, "No man or God would be able to kill you. You can only be killed by a woman."

Parvati's face started glowing. The glow took the form of a bright light. That light took the shape of a Goddess with several hands. In each of her hands was

a weapon and she was astride a lion given to her by the mountain God, Himalayas. Astride the lion, the devi began to roar.

Mahishasura or Durg sent soldiers to kill her. The Goddess was not bothered. With a blow of air from her cheeks, she reduced the huddle of attacking soldiers to ashes!

The Goddess or Devi then caught Durg in a noose. Durg then assumed the shape of a lion. The Devi chopped the Lion's head.

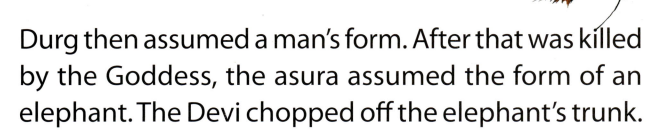

Durg then assumed a man's form. After that was killed by the Goddess, the asura assumed the form of an elephant. The Devi chopped off the elephant's trunk.

Durg then assumed the form of a buffalo. Assuming the shape of a wild buffalo and using his hooves, tail and mouth, Durg attacked the Goddess. Suddenly, the Devi jumped on Mahisha's

back. With one foot she pressed down his throat and pushed her trident into Durg. Durg assuming his demon form, emerged from the buffalo. Using her sword, the devi then chopped off Durg's head and he died.

Parvati was given the name Durga, *because she killed Durg,* better known as Mahishasura. Goddess Durga is worshipped during an annual festival called Durga Puja, especially popular among Bengalis.

BRAHMA'S LIE

Long ago, there was a moment when Brahma, the creator and Vishnu, the preserver, got into a loud argument.

"It is I who is superior," stormed Lord Brahma, floating on his swan in the skies. Lord Vishnu laughed and dismissed this claim, "You know, it is not true. It is I who is the superior one between you and me."

The heated argument was so fierce that the celestial kingdom of the Gods shook with this war of words!

The other Gods were worried and went to Lord Shiva, the destroyer. "They are quarrelling about who is superior of the two. Please do something," they begged Shiva. Assuming the form of an unending column of fire, Shiva appeared in the middle of the conflicting duo. Brahma and Vishnu were taken aback, as they didn't realize what had come between them.

"The one who finds the beginning and the end of this column shall be declared superior," came instructions from the fiery, swaying, brilliant pillar of light. The two disputing Gods looked up the pillar of fire, but there was no top visible. They looked down and there was no bottom.

They decided to take the challenge. Brahma flew upwards on his swan tracing the top of the column. Vishnu went into the earth tracking the end of the column. Thousands of miles and many years of travel later, both the Gods were unsuccessful in their pursuit. During his futile search, Brahma came across a Ketaki flower.

"I was at the top. Someone had laid me as an offering! I have fallen down," Ketaki blinked. Picking up Ketaki, Brahma looked up but there was no top and he knew she was lying. But he decided to tell a small white lie himself! Returning, Brahma heard Vishnu confessing that he had not found the end of the column.

"I have," announced Brahma. "This is Ketaki. She is my witness." Oh no, Brahma had let ego guide his decision. An enraged Shiva caught his lie. Manifesting himself back to his true form, he admonished Brahma. Feeling very embarrassed, Brahma admitted that he had lied. "No one shall pray to you. No one will offer Ketaki as a flower to the Gods. She lied and gave a false testimony," Shiva declared. Hence, it is not surprising that Brahma is not widely worshipped and there are no temples for Brahma except for one in Rajasthan.

HANUMAN GETS THE SACRED HERB

During the battle of Lanka between Ram and Ravan, Meghnath shot a powerful weapon at Lakshman.

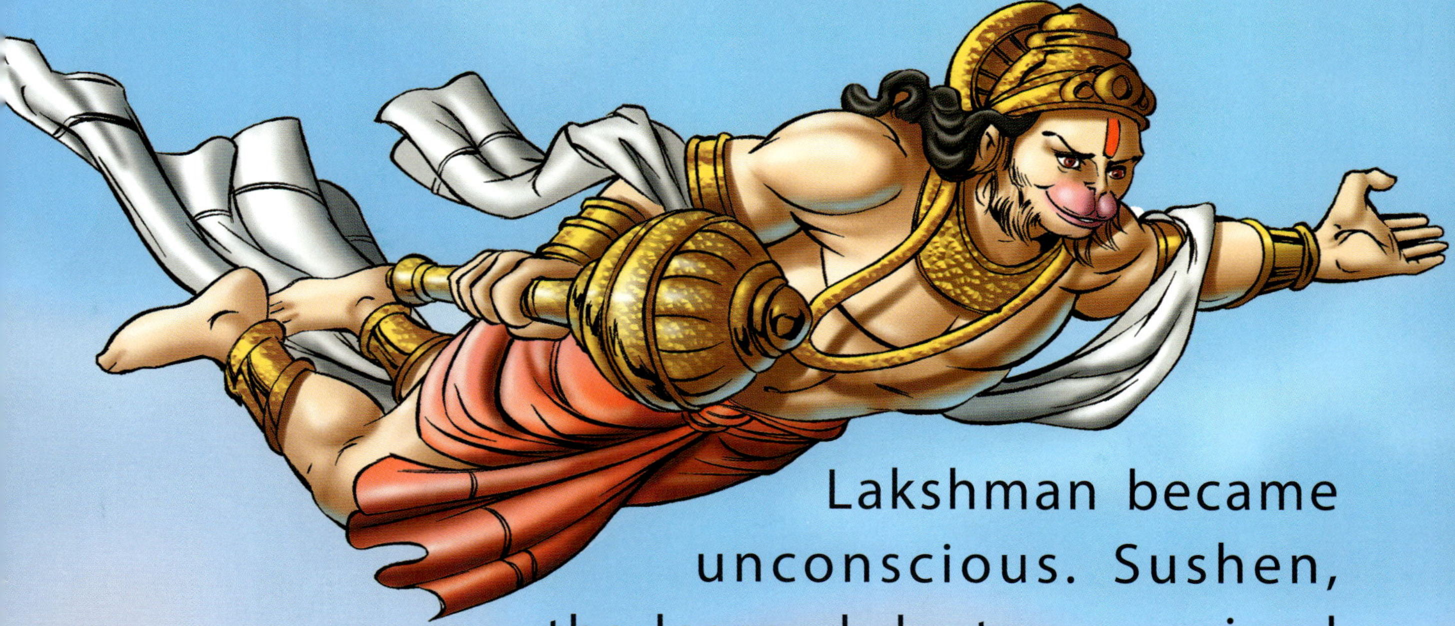

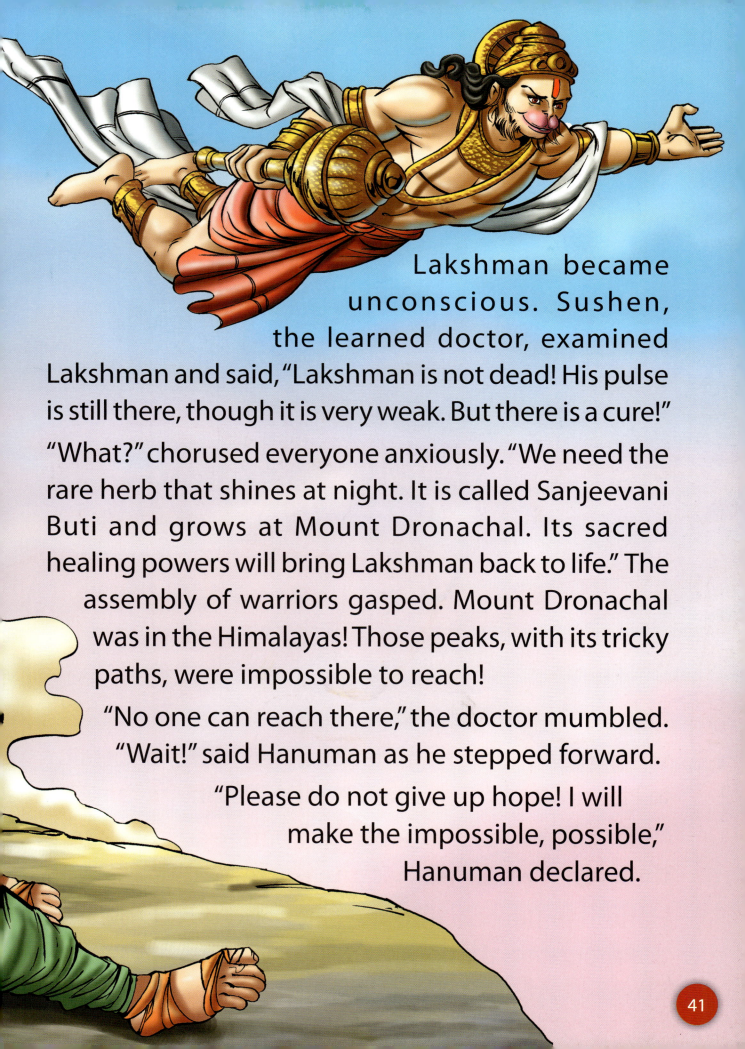

Lakshman became unconscious. Sushen, the learned doctor, examined Lakshman and said, "Lakshman is not dead! His pulse is still there, though it is very weak. But there is a cure!"

"What?" chorused everyone anxiously. "We need the rare herb that shines at night. It is called Sanjeevani Buti and grows at Mount Dronachal. Its sacred healing powers will bring Lakshman back to life." The assembly of warriors gasped. Mount Dronachal was in the Himalayas! Those peaks, with its tricky paths, were impossible to reach!

"No one can reach there," the doctor mumbled. "Wait!" said Hanuman as he stepped forward. "Please do not give up hope! I will make the impossible, possible," Hanuman declared.

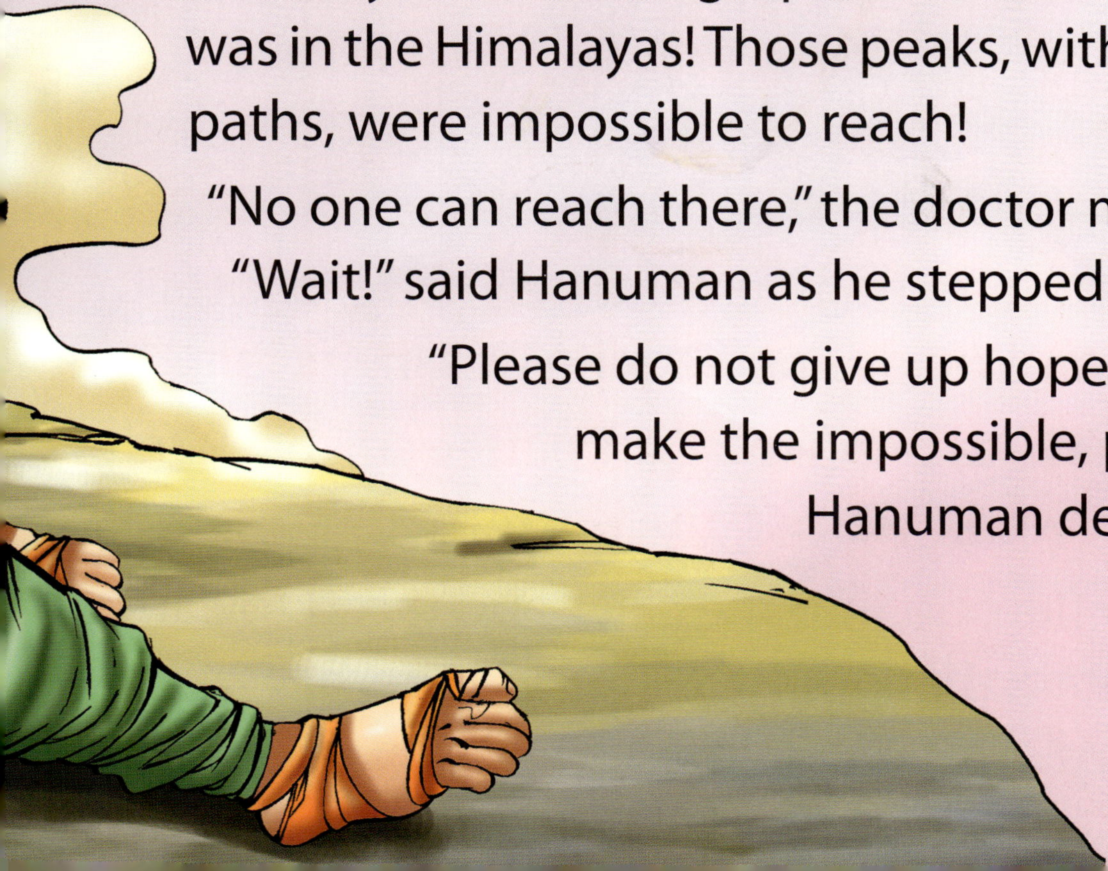

Everyone nodded in agreement. They had explicit faith in Hanuman. With his powers, he was invincible.

"But you have to bring the 'buti' before sun rise! Only then will it work," warned the doctor.

Hanuman flew up into the skies and raced towards the mountain that grew the precious herb.

Meanwhile, **King Ravan** came to know of all these happenings.

Ravan thought of a plan to stop Hanuman and announced,

"Call Surya, I will ask him to rise at midnight."

"At midnight, why?" gulped the dumbfounded courtiers.

"Early sunrise means less time for Hanuman to get the buti. That means Lakshman will not get a cure! Ha–ha–ha–ha!"

Soon, Surya presented himself before Ravan.

"Yes, king Ravan?" Lord Surya sighed resignedly.

"Rise at midnight, Lord Surya!"

"As you say, king Ravan," sighed Surya again.

Ravan was very powerful, thus Surya had to comply to his wish.

Very sullen and forced to obey, Surya sailed back to his repose but not before grumbling,

"Waking up at midnight! I hate that!"

In the interim, Hanuman sailed strongly towards the Himalayas. "Aha, I see the peaks! But what is this? Is the sun rising? It is only midnight?" Hanuman's mind quizzed.

"I get it! It is that evil Ravan who is creating this hurdle," Hanuman realized. With a push of air currents, Hanuman turned course and spurred towards the sun.

The sun was lazily rising. But as soon as it saw Hanuman racing towards him, the sun croaked, "Hanuman, don't…I am forced to do this…hey, hey!"

The sun tried to run! With one engulfing gasp, Hanuman caught the sun and hooked it tightly under his armpit so that no sunlight could escape at all.

"You will rise on your time! You will stay with me till my task is done and over!"

"Ok!" came a muffled reply from the sun, nicely ensconced under Hanuman's arm! Hanuman then dashed to Mount Dronachal. He landed on the top of the mountain and stared.

"All the herbs are shining? Which one is the sacred 'buti'?" Hanuman paced up and down.

The sun whimpered,

"Hanuman, time is finishing! Hurry–hurry! We have to return!"

With an abrupt chortle, he suddenly announced, "I shall carry the entire mountain to Sushen and he can choose the herb himself!"

The sun said, "Good idea! Moreover, you are *Bajrangbali* or the one who has the strength of the thunderbolts! You can do anything!"

"Thank you for saying so, Lord Surya! Now sit settled! I have work to do," Hanuman chuckled. Then with a huge breath, Hanuman flexed his powerful muscles and reached out for the base of Mount Dronachal.

"Arrrrrrrgh! Whoooosh! WenchHHHHH!" Hanuman scrunched his face and applied his force to loosen the mountain! The mountain went "tearrrrrrrrrrrrr!" Himalayas trembled. Hanuman did not stop and instantly uprooted the mountain!

Then he raced back to Lakshman. He reached amongst great relief. Sushen immediately identified the herb. As soon as the cure was applied on Lakshman, he woke up immediately.